Wonders

Mc
Graw
Hill
Education

Cover and Title Page: Nathan Love

www.mheonline.com/readingwonders

Mc Graw Hill Education

Copyright © 2017 McGraw-Hill Education

Send all inquiries to:
McGraw-Hill Education
2 Penn Plaza
New York, NY 10121

ISBN: 978-0-02-131116-3
MHID: 0-02-131116-1

Printed in the United States of America.

9 LKV 27 26 25   D

Wonders

ELD
Companion Worktext

Program Authors

Diane August

Jana Echevarria

Josefina V. Tinajero

McGraw Hill Education

Unit 6

Linked In

1

Linked In

The Big Idea

How are we all connected?

? Essential Question

How do different groups contribute to a cause?

>> *Go Digital*

4

COLLABORATE What are the women doing? Why are they building airplanes? How did they contribute, or help, to the cause of the war effort? How can people contribute to a cause? Write words in the chart.

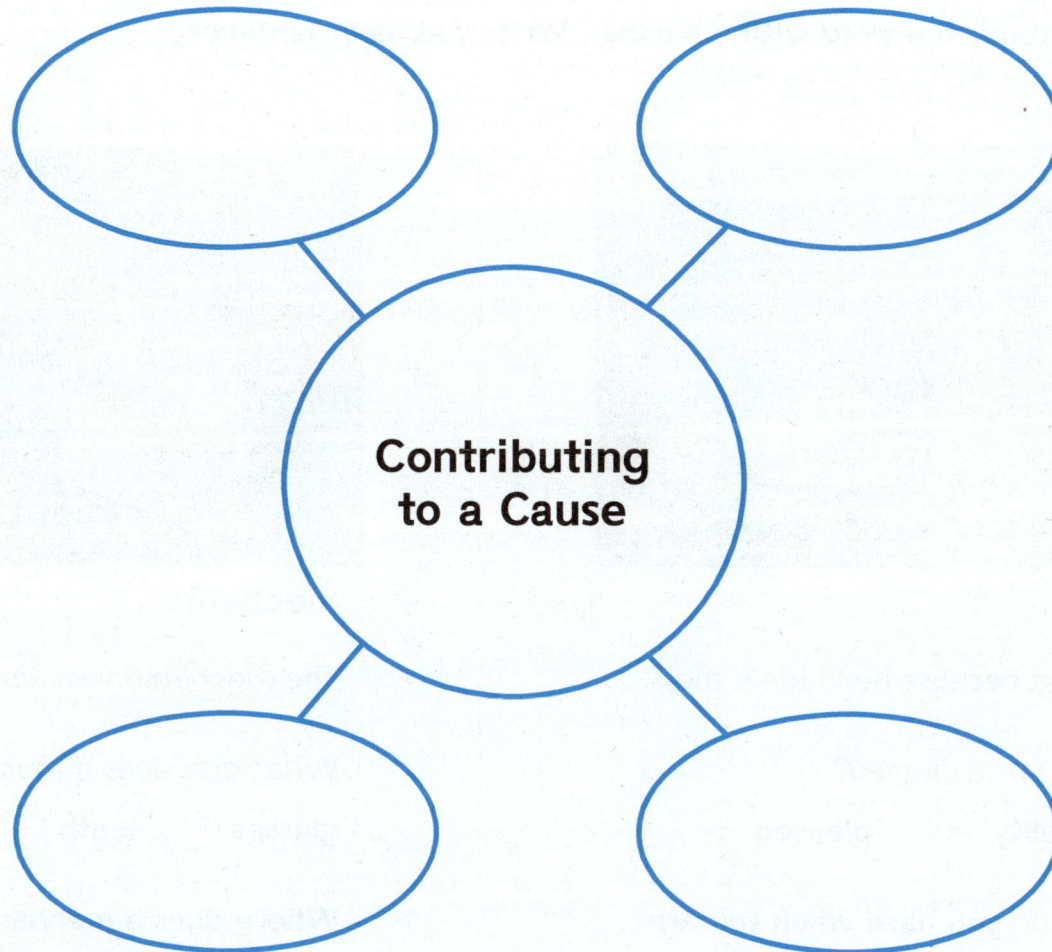

Contributing to a Cause

Discuss how people can contribute to a cause. Use words from the chart. You can say:

Women contributed to the cause of the war effort by _____.

People can contribute to a cause by _____.

More Vocabulary

Look at the picture. Read the word. Then read the sentence. Talk about the word with a partner. Write your own sentence.

ashamed

Seth is **ashamed** because he made a mess.

What word means *ashamed*?

angry   **guilty**   **pleased**

What feelings do you have when you are ashamed?

When I am ashamed, I feel _____

_____.

mechanic

The **mechanic** fixes the engine.

What else does a *mechanic* fix?

glasses   **tooth**   **motorcycle**

Where does a mechanic work?

A mechanic works at a _____

_____.

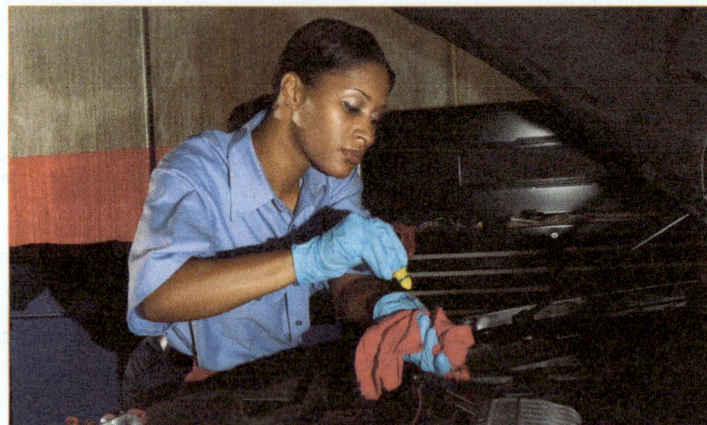

Eclipse Studios/McGraw-Hill Education; Jupiterimages/Comstock Images/Getty Images

Words and Phrases: *hear* and *here*

Homophones

The words *hear* and *here* are homophones. Homophones sound the same, but they have different spellings and meanings.

The word *hear* means "listen to someone or something."

Do the boys know what the girl is whispering?

No, the boys cannot **hear** the whispers.

The word *here* means "in this place."

Where is the city located on the map?

The city is located **here**.

COLLABORATE **Look at the picture. Read the sentence. Talk with a partner. Write the word that completes each sentence.**

Chandie arrived on the school bus.

She is _____ now.

     hear   **here**

Did Uncle Nick _____ the visitors ring the doorbell?

     hear   **here**

COLLABORATE

1 Talk About It

Look at the picture. Read the title. Talk about what you see. Use these words.

flag   building   bakery   signs

Write about what you see.

This story is about _____

_____

_____.

What do you see in the store window?

I see _____

_____

_____.

What is above the store?

There is _____

_____.

Take notes as you read the story.

SHIPPED OUT

Essential Question

? How do different groups contribute to a cause?

Read about how a young girl contributes to the war effort.

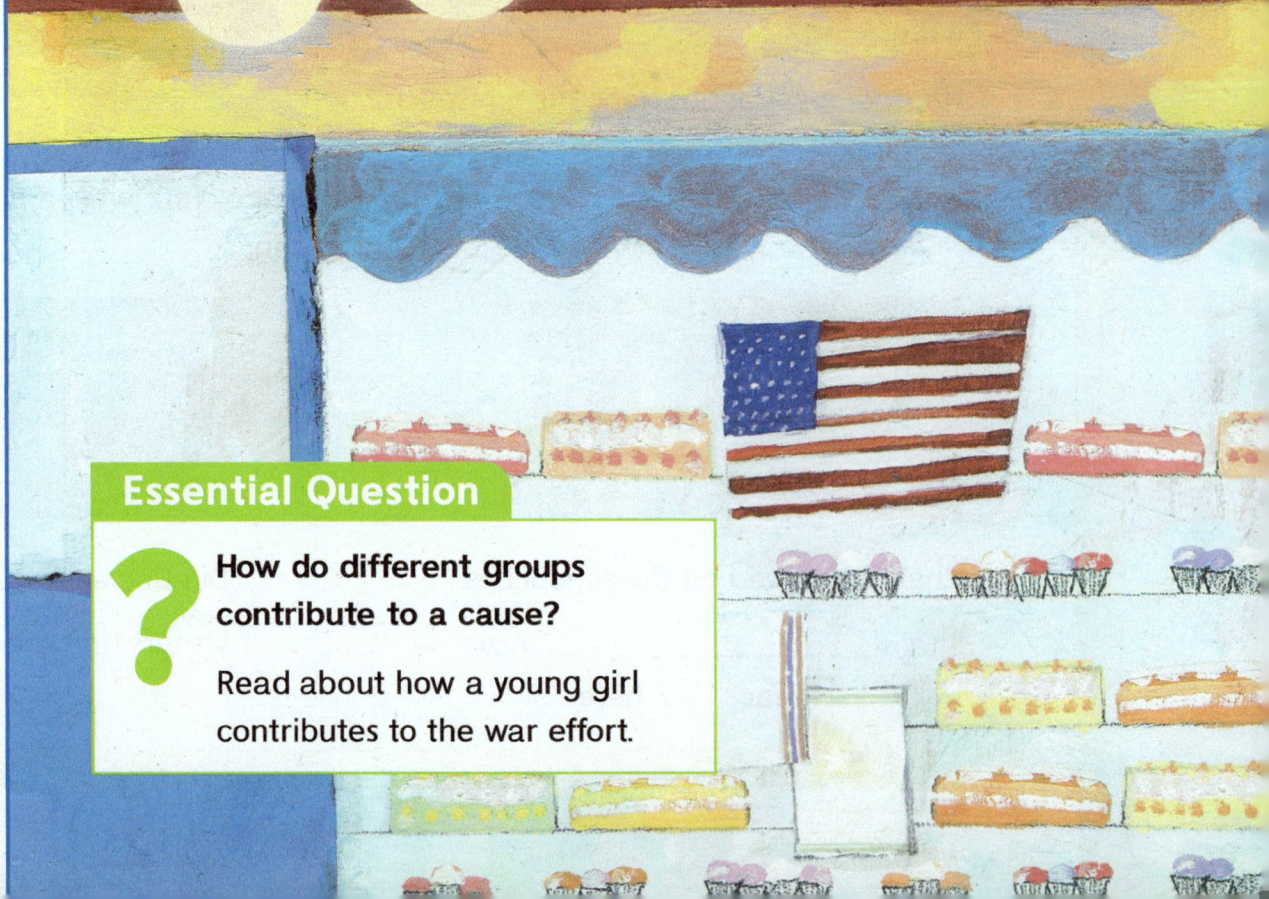

My name is Libby Kendall. Some days I feel like I am a prisoner of war. Just like my dad, I packed my bags and shipped out. Unlike my dad, I can't help the Allies win World War II.

My father is a **mechanic** on a battleship in the Pacific Ocean, so Mom and I moved to an apartment above Aunt Lucia's bakery. Mom works at the clothing factory. She sews pockets on uniforms. I asked if she snuck poetry in the pockets for soldiers to find. She said soldiers wore jackets with pockets to hold tools they might need for war survival, not silly things like poetry.

I help Aunt Lucia in the bakery since her workers joined the army. We get up before dawn to knead the dough. Next, we bake breads and muffins. Then, while I help customers, Lucia makes cakes and cookies. Lucia answers all the phone calls. She worries that it might be bad news, so she wants to be the first to know.

After dinner, her neighbors come over to listen to the radio. Lucia and others translate the news for some of the neighbors who don't speak English. I always listen for news about the fighting in the Pacific.

Sean Qualls

1 Specific Vocabulary A C T

The phrase *Just like* means "in the same way." What word has an opposite meaning? Underline the word in the next sentence. How is Libby just like her dad?

Just like Dad, Libby _____

_____.

2 Sentence Structure A C T

Reread the last sentence in the third paragraph. The word *might* tells about a possible event. Circle the possible event. What is Aunt Lucia worried about?

She is worried _____

_____.

3 Comprehension Theme

Reread the last paragraph. How does Aunt Lucia help her neighbors? Put a box around the text.

1 Specific Vocabulary ⒶⒸⓉ

The phrase *face grew hot* means "became angry." What does Libby do to show her anger? Underline the text that tells you.

To show her anger, Libby _____

_____.

2 Sentence Structure ⒶⒸⓉ

Reread the last sentence of the third paragraph. What does Libby look back on? Circle the text in the paragraph that tells you. How does Libby feel now?

Now Libby feels _____

_____.

3 Comprehension

Reread the last paragraph. Why does Aunt Lucia ask Libby to help make cupcakes? Circle the text.

Aunt Lucia's reason is _____

_____.

I remember how my parents used to read about the war. They often whispered so I couldn't hear them.

One night, my parents shared what they had been talking about. Dad said, "Our country's at war. The military is looking for new recruits. I intend to join the navy because I know about boats and ship engines."

My face grew hot. "You can't just leave," I said. I stomped down the hall to my bedroom.

Looking back on that, I feel **ashamed** of how selfish I was.

This morning, Aunt Lucia can tell I'm feeling down, so she asks me to help her make cupcakes for a fundraiser. At first, I'm not interested. I slather frosting on the top. Then I realize I can make red stripes with strawberries and a patch of blue with blueberries. Soon I have a tray of cupcakes decorated like American flags.

Sean Qualls

"Your cupcakes are wonderful! They'll sell better than anything else!" Lucia says.

I feel like I've done something right. I think about all the money we might make at the sale and how it may help my father.

Before Dad left, he explained, "I enlisted in the navy to help restore democracy in the world." He told me, "Now you be good, young lady." I promised him I would. As he left, I slipped a poem into his coat pocket. The poem said, "Here is a little rhyme to pass the day. I love you back in the U.S.A.!"

I look at the platter of cupcakes and wish I could send them to Dad. Instead, I'll draw a picture of them and send it to the Pacific. Then, Dad will have plenty to share with everyone there.

Make Connections

? What contributions to the war effort do characters make in the story?
ESSENTIAL QUESTION

Think about a time when you needed people's help. How did you work together?
TEXT TO SELF

Text Evidence

COLLABORATE

1 Talk About It

Discuss why people have fundraisers. How can Libby help her father by selling cupcakes?

2 Sentence Structure A C T

Reread the second and third sentences in the third paragraph. What does Libby promise her dad? Circle the text that tells you.

Libby promises her dad _____

_____.

3 Comprehension
Theme

Reread the last paragraph. Underline Libby's actions. How do her actions help the war effort?

Libby's actions help the war effort

because _____

_____.

Respond to the Text

Partner Discussion Work with a partner. Read the questions about "Shipped Out." Show where you found text evidence. Write the page numbers. Then discuss what you read.

How does Libby's family help with the war effort?

I read that Libby's dad joined _____.

Libby's mom works at _____.

Aunt Lucia has a fundraiser to _____.

Text Evidence 🔍

Page(s): _____

Page(s): _____

Page(s): _____

How does Libby help with the war effort?

Libby helps her aunt by _____.

For the fundraiser, Libby makes _____.

Libby sends her dad _____

_____.

Text Evidence 🔍

Page(s): _____

Page(s): _____

Page(s): _____

Group Discussion Present your answers to the group. Cite text evidence for your ideas. Listen to and discuss the group's opinions.

Write Work with a partner. Look at your notes about "Shipped Out." Write your answer to the Essential Question. Use text evidence to support your answer. Use vocabulary words in your writing.

How do Libby and her family help the war effort?

Each person _____ the war effort differently.

Dad joins _____.

Mom sews _____.

Libby and Aunt Lucia work together to _____

_____.

Libby draws _____

_____.

Share Writing Present your writing to the class. Discuss their opinions. Talk about their ideas. You can say:

I agree with _____.

I do not agree because _____.

Write to Sources

Take Notes About the Text I took notes about the text on the chart to respond to the prompt: *Add a new event to the story. Write about Libby's family before her dad joined the navy.*

pages 8–11

Text Clue	New Event
Libby's father is a mechanic on a ship.	Libby's father was a mechanic before the war.
Mom and Libby moved to Aunt Lucia's apartment.	Libby's family lived together near Aunt Lucia.
Mom works at the factory. She will work for few months.	Mom did not work before the war.
Aunt Lucia's workers joined the army. Libby works at the bakery.	Libby went to the bakery with her parents.
Libby was upset when Dad told her he joined the navy.	Libby and her Dad spent time together before the war.

Write About the Text I used notes from my chart to write a paragraph about Libby's family before the war.

Student Model: *Narrative Text*

Life was different before the war. Libby's father was a mechanic. He fixed engines on cars, buses, and motorcycles. Libby and her parents lived in an apartment near Aunt Lucia. They visited Aunt Lucia's bakery. Libby ate bread, and her parents talked to Aunt Lucia. Libby's mom didn't work. Libby's father didn't work on weekends. The family did a lot of things together. Then Libby's father joined the navy. Libby was very upset.

TALK ABOUT IT

Text Evidence
Draw a box around a sentence that comes from the notes. Which text clue did Roberto use to write the sentence?

Grammar
Circle the two prepositional phrases in the third sentence. What do they describe?

Connect Ideas
Underline the two sentences that tell about when Libby's father joined the navy. How can you use the word *because* to connect the sentences?

Your Turn
Add a new event. Write about what happens when Libby receives a letter from her father. Use text evidence in your writing.

>> Go Digital!
Write your response online. Use your editing checklist.

Weekly Concept Getting Along

? Essential Question

What actions can we take to get along with others?

>> *Go Digital*

What does the photograph show? How do you know the animals are getting along? What do people do to get along? Write words in the chart.

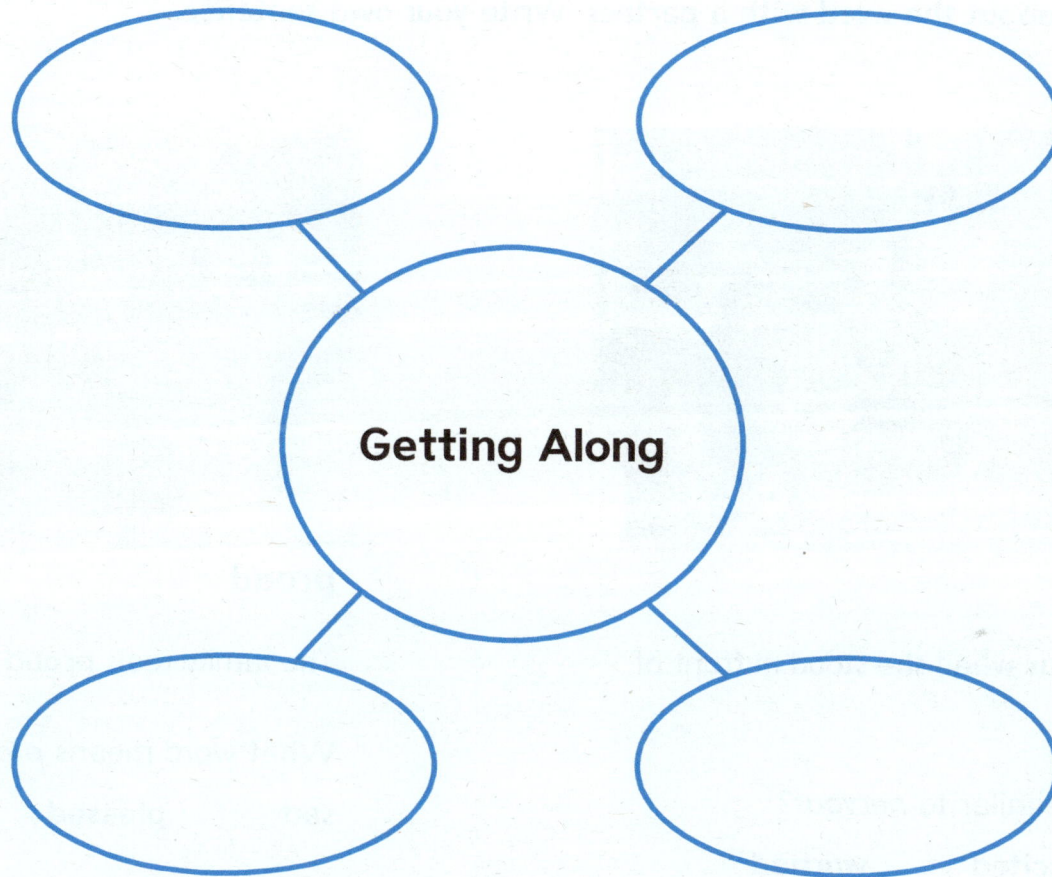

Getting Along

Discuss what people do to get along. Use words from the chart. Complete the sentences.

I know that the animals are getting along because _____

_____.

People get along by _____.

More Vocabulary

COLLABORATE Look at the picture. Read the word. Then read the sentence.
Talk about the word with a partner. Write your own sentence.

nervous

Ana felt **nervous** when she stood in front of the class.

What word is similar to *nervous*?

upset   **excited**   **worried**

When do you feel nervous?

I feel nervous when I _____.

proud

The family feels **proud** of Tyler's award.

What word means *proud*?

sad   **pleased**   **tired**

When are you proud of yourself?

I am proud of myself when I _____.

18

Words and Phrases: *whenever* and *yet*

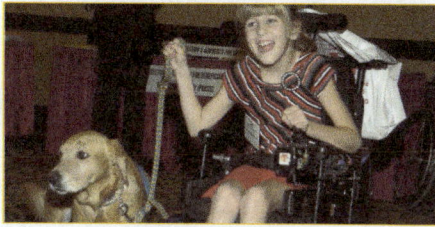

The word *whenever* means "any time something happens."

When does the dog follow Jenna?

The dog follows Jenna **whenever** she holds the leash.

One meaning of the word *yet* is "but."

Did the team win?

No, the team lost. **Yet,** they played well.

COLLABORATE **Look at the picture. Read the sentence. Talk with a partner. Write the word that completes each sentence.**

The children like school, _____

they are happy to start their vacation.

    whenever   **yet**

_____ it rains, the bird

bath fills with water.

    Whenever   **Yet**

COLLABORATE

1 Talk About It

Look at the picture. Read the title. Talk about what you see. Use these words.

scare   bully   hallway   stare

Write about what you see.

This story is about a _____

_____.

Who is the bully in the picture?

The bully is _____

_____.

What is the bully doing in the picture?

He is _____

_____.

Take notes as you read the story.

The Bully

Essential Question

?   **What actions can we take to get along with others?**

Read about how a student deals with a bully.

Michael saw J.T. standing at the end of the hallway. J. T. was the school bully. He was tall and strong, so kids were afraid to stand up to him. Michael didn't like the way J. T. acted. Yet just like the other kids who get picked on, Michael didn't complain.

J.T. walked toward Michael and stared at the books Michael carried under his arms. As they passed each other, J.T. stopped suddenly. Then he snapped at Michael, "Hey, let me see those books!" Michael held out the book and tried not to tremble. He didn't want to reveal how nervous he was.

The other kids watched as J.T. grabbed Michael's math book. Then he shoved the book back at Michael, who dropped the rest of his books. J.T. barked, "Pick up your books!" Then he walked away laughing loudly.

Michael half kicked his books. Suddenly, someone handed Michael one of his books. He heard a friendly voice say, "You look like you could use an ally."

Marcelo Baez

Text Evidence

1 Specific Vocabulary A C T

The word *snapped* means "to say something quickly and angrily." Circle a word with similar meaning in the third paragraph. Why did J.T. snap at Michael?

J.T. snapped at Michael because

_____

2 Sentence Structure A C T

Reread the second sentence of the third paragraph. What caused Michael to drop his books? Underline the text that tells you.

Michael dropped his books because

_____.

3 Comprehension

Reread the third paragraph. Put a box around the words that describe the actions of a bully. Write about it.

A bully _____

_____.

1 Sentence Structure Ⓐ Ⓒ Ⓣ

Reread fourth and fifth paragraphs. The pronouns *that* and *It* refer to the same thing. Underline the text that tells you in the third paragraph.

The pronouns refer to _____

_____.

2 Comprehension

Reread the sixth paragraph. Put a box around Michael's suggestion. Why does he make the suggestion?

Michael makes the suggestion

because _____

_____.

COLLABORATE

3 Talk About It

Reread the seventh paragraph. Discuss why Ramon says Michael's suggestion is vinegar. Support your answer with text evidence.

Michael looked up and saw Ramon, the star baseball and basketball player. Michael was surprised. They had not talked to each other since the beginning of the school year.

"Thanks," Michael sighed with relief. "It's so confusing. I don't know what his problem is."

Ramon responded, "Well, you need to find a way to end the conflict with J.T." He continued, "I'll tell you what my grandmother used to tell me whenever I had a problem with someone. She'd say, 'You can catch more flies with honey than with vinegar.'"

Michael asked, "What does that mean?"

"It means that being kind to your enemies is better than being angry," Ramon explained.

"What if you just intervene and tell J.T. to stop picking on me?" Michael suggested. "He won't bully me if you threatened him."

"That's vinegar," Ramon laughed. "Try honey instead."

That night, Michael thought about Ramon's advice. It sounded like a good plan, but will it work?

The next day in school Michael saw J.T. and felt terrible. He knew what was going to happen.

Marcelo Baez

Michael got nervous as J.T. came nearer. Then, the unexpected happened. J.T. accidentally tripped. He fell down and his books went flying across the floor.

For a moment, all was silent. The crowd of students in the hallway froze, waiting to see what J.T. would do next. As J.T. stood up slowly, Michael had an idea. He bent down, picked up J.T.'s books, and offered the books to him.

Michael said, "You look like you could use an ally."

J.T. was speechless, confused by Michael's act of kindness. He took the books and muttered quickly, "Uh, thanks."

As J.T. walked away, Ramon gave Michael a big smile. Ramon said, "My grandmother would be proud of you."

Michael grinned, "It's just honey. I hope it sticks."

Make Connections

? Talk about how Ramon helps Michael. **ESSENTIAL QUESTION**

What advice would you give to someone being bullied? Give reasons to support your opinion. **TEXT TO SELF**

Text Evidence

1 Sentence Structure A C T

Reread the last sentence in the first paragraph. Circle the reason the books flew across the floor.

2 Specific Vocabulary A C T

The word *speechless* has the suffix *-less*, which means "without or not." Write the meaning of speechless. Why is J.T. speechless? Underline the reason.

The word speechless means _____

_____.

3 Comprehension
Theme

Reread the fifth paragraph. Why would Ramon's grandmother be proud of Michael? Underline text that tells you in the second paragraph.

Ramon's grandmother would

be proud because _____

_____.

Respond to the Text

Partner Discussion Work with a partner. Read the questions about "The Bully." Show where you found text evidence. Write the page numbers. Then discuss what you read.

Why didn't Michael and J.T. get along?

J.T. was the school _____.

J.T. shoved Michael's _____.

This made Michael _____.

Text Evidence

Page(s): _____

Page(s): _____

Page(s): _____

How did Ramon help Michael?

Ramon told Michael what his grandmother told him. She said _____

_____.

Michael helped J.T. when he _____.

Ramon was proud of Michael because _____

_____.

Text Evidence

Page(s): _____

Page(s): _____

Page(s): _____

Group Discussion Present your answers to the group. Cite text evidence for your ideas. Listen to and discuss the group's opinions.

Write Work with a partner. Look at your notes about "The Bully." Write your answer to the Essential Question. Use text evidence to support your answer. Use vocabulary words in your writing.

What did Michael do to get along with J.T.?

J.T. was a bully, so Michael felt _____.

Ramon suggested to Michael to _____

_____.

When J. T. needed help, Michael _____

_____.

Michael realized that _____

_____.

Share Writing Present your writing to the class. Discuss their opinions. Talk about their ideas. You can say:

I agree with _____.

I do not agree because _____.

Paco

Take Notes About the Text I took notes about the text on the chart to answer the question: *Should Ramon have stopped J. T. from bullying Michael? Write your opinion.*

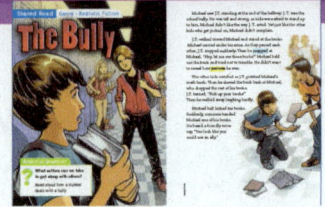

pages 20–23

Text Evidence	Conclusion
Ramon is a star baseball and basketball player.	Ramon is strong and popular. J.T. will listen to Ramon.
Ramon tells Michael to be kind to your enemies.	Ramon thinks Michael should be kind to J.T.
Michael wants Ramon to threaten J. T. Ramon says no. Ramon tells Michael to be kind.	Ramon thinks Michael needs to solve the problem.
J. T. trips in the hallway. Michael is kind to J. T. and J.T. does not bully Michael.	Michael solves his problem by himself.

Write About the Text I used notes from my chart to write an opinion about Ramon.

Student Model: *Opinion*

I think Ramon helped Michael to solve his problem by himself. Ramon is strong and popular. J. T. probably would listen to Ramon. However, Ramon told Michael to be kind to your enemies. Ramon probably thought Michael can solve his problem with J.T. Ramon did not speak out for him. In the end, Michael was kind to J.T., and J.T. did not bully him. Michael solved his problem by himself.

TALK ABOUT IT

COLLABORATE

Text Evidence

Draw a box around a sentence that comes from the notes. Did Paco use the information to tell his opinion?

Grammar

Circle the reflexive pronoun in the first sentence. How is a reflexive pronoun different from other pronouns?

Connect Ideas

Underline the second and third sentences. How can you use *because* to combine the sentences and connect the ideas?

Your Turn

COLLABORATE

In your opinion, will J. T. be nice to Michael in the future? Use text evidence in your writing.

>> Go Digital!
Write your response online. Use your editing checklist.

Weekly Concept Adaptations

Essential Question

How are living things adapted to their environment?

>> *Go Digital*

What does the lizard have all over its body? How do the thorns help the lizard survive? What adaptations do animals and people have? Write words in the chart.

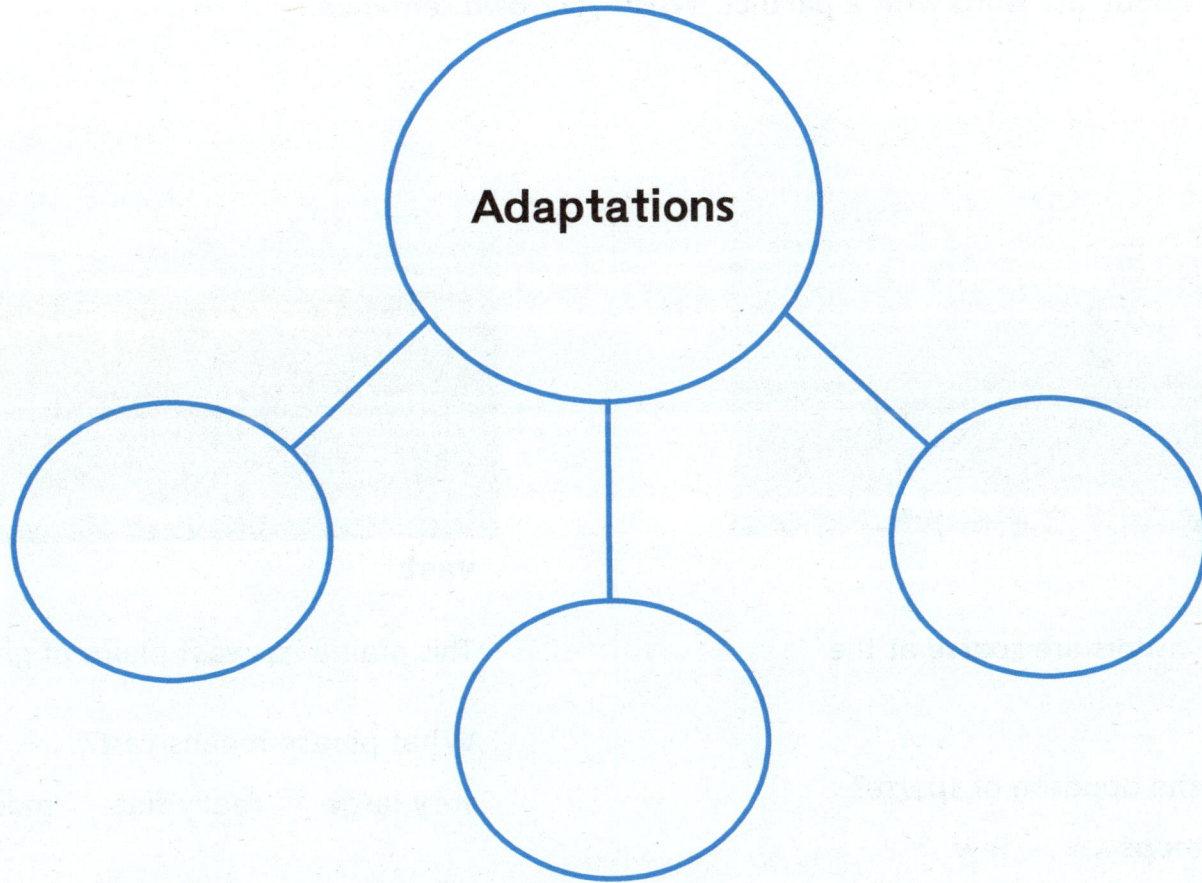

Adaptations

Discuss the adaptations animals and people have. Use words from the chart. Complete the sentences.

The thorns help the lizard to _____.

Animals have _____

to adapt to the environment.

More Vocabulary

COLLABORATE Look at the picture. Read the word. Then read the sentence. Talk about the word with a partner. Write your own sentence.

sparse

On chilly days, visitors are sparse at the beach.

What word is the opposite of *sparse*?

many   **groups**   **few**

When are leaves on trees sparse?

Leaves are sparse on trees during

_____.

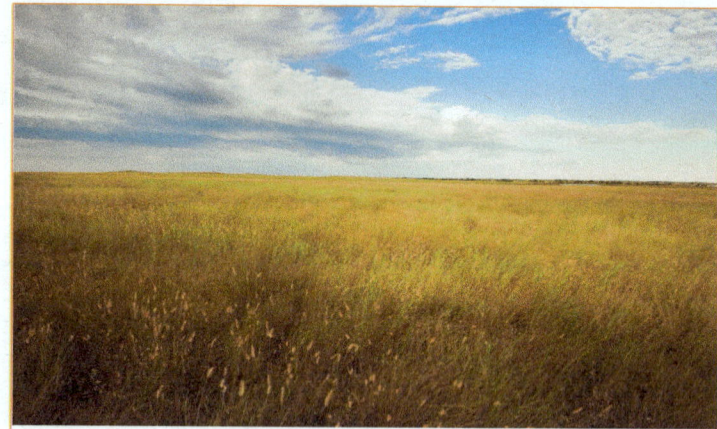

vast

This prairie has vast plains of grass.

What phrase means *vast*?

very large   **really flat**   **mostly green**

Why is an ocean vast?

An ocean is vast because _____

_____.

30

Words and Phrases: *in addition to* and *just as*

The phrase *in addition to* means "along with" or "together with."

What does Patti eat for breakfast?

In addition to fruit, Patti eats toast.

The phrase *just as* means "in the same way as."

What does Felicia play?

Felicia plays guitar, **just as** her father does.

COLLABORATE **Look at the picture. Read the sentence. Talk with a partner. Write the phrase that completes each sentence.**

Kristen is good at jump rope,

_____ Monica is.

in addition to   just as

The boy camps with a lantern

_____ a sleeping bag.

in addition to   just as

COLLABORATE

1 Talk About It

Look at the photograph. Read the title. Discuss what you see. Use these words.

fish   tube worm   deep   swim

Write about what you see.

The text is about _____

_____.

What does the photograph show?

The photograph shows _____

_____

_____.

What does the caption tell you about the photograph?

The caption tells me that _____

_____

_____.

Take notes as you read the text.

Mysterious Oceans

Essential Question

? **How are living things adapted to their environment?**

Read about how sea creatures adapted to the deep ocean.

Emory Kristof/National Geographic Stock

Deep Diving

It has no mouth, eyes, or stomach. Its soft body is in a white cylinder. It has a red top and can grow to be eight feet tall. It is a giant tube worm and it lives on the deep, dark ocean floor.

Oceans cover about two-thirds of Earth's surface. On average, oceans are about two miles deep. However, the deepest point is nearly seven miles deep. It is called Challenger Deep.

The ocean's floor has **vast** plains, steep canyons, and towering mountains. There are active, dormant, and extinct volcanoes. The environment is harsh because it has frigid temperatures and no sunshine.

The deep ocean is a **mystery**. We know little about it. For example, we knew giant squids existed from discovering their corpses. We finally found a live giant squid just a few years ago.

◀ Some fish swim among tube worms in the deep ocean.

The Challenger Deep is located in a canyon called the Mariana Trench.

The Deepest Known Point on Earth

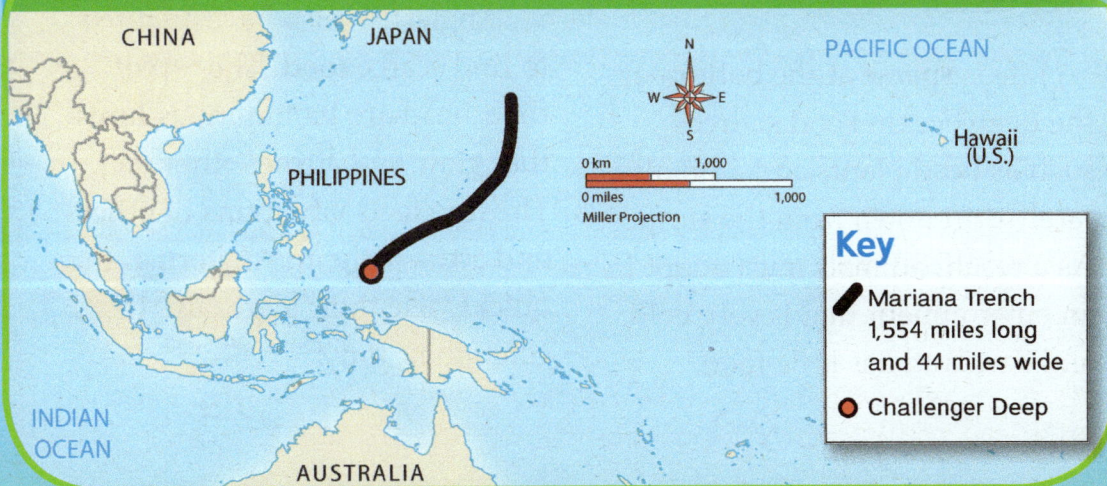

CHINA JAPAN PACIFIC OCEAN

PHILIPPINES

Hawaii (U.S.)

N W E S

0 km 1,000
0 miles 1,000
Miller Projection

Key

▬ Mariana Trench 1,554 miles long and 44 miles wide

● Challenger Deep

INDIAN OCEAN

AUSTRALIA

Text Evidence 🔍

1 Sentence Structure Ⓐ Ⓒ Ⓣ

Reread the first paragraph. Underline the text that the pronoun *it* refers to. What does it look like? Write about it.

_____

_____

2 Comprehension
Cause and Effect

Reread the last sentence of the third paragraph. The word *because* signals a cause. Circle the effect in the sentence.

The effect is _____

_____.

3 Specific Vocabulary Ⓐ Ⓒ Ⓣ

The word *mystery* means "something that is not understood" Put a box around the word that tells this meaning.

The deep ocean is a mystery

because _____.

33

Text Evidence

1 Sentence Structure ACT

Reread the second sentence in the second paragraph. Underline the text that tells examples of food sources. What are food sources used for?

They are used for _____

_____.

2 Specific Vocabulary ACT

Lures attract fish so they can be caught. Circle context clues that help you figure out the meaning of lure. Why is a lure an adaptation?

A lure is an adaptation because

_____

_____.

COLLABORATE

3 Talk About It

Describe examples of adaptation to the environment in the deep ocean. Use text evidence to explain.

This frogfish lures prey with its nose.

A basket starfish rests in a reef.

Amazing Adaptations

A submersible, or submarine, is a craft that goes underwater. The submersible allows scientists to explore the deep ocean floor. However, exploration remains difficult, and scientists have explored only five percent of the deep ocean.

Life is **sparse** at the bottom of the deep ocean. Food sources, such as dead plants and animals, rarely drift down from the surface. As a result, animals must adapt to an environment that is very cold and dark and has little food.

One example of an adaptation to this environment is the deep sea starfish. They grow larger and more aggressive than the starfish in shallow waters. Deep sea starfish are predators. They reach up with their five arms to catch and eat shrimp.

Anglerfish also have adapted to find scarce food. The top of their head are bioluminous **lures** that glow and attract other fish. The lure feels vibrations of others and attracts them. Anglerfish then quickly use their huge jaws to catch their prey.

(l) Pixtal/AGE Fotostock; (r) Lophelia II 2009 Expedition, NOAA-OER

Heated Habitats

One surprising discovery was that cracks, or vents, appear on the deep ocean floor, just as they do on dry land. Sea water rushes into the vents and mixes with chemicals. Next, magma, or hot melted rock, heats the water. Then the water bursts back into the ocean and creates geysers and hot springs.

Surprisingly, the waters around these vents **teem** with life. In addition to tube worms, there are huge clams, eyeless shrimp, crabs, mussels, and many kinds of bacteria. One odd creature is the Pompeii worm. Bacteria cover the back of the worm and insulate it from heat.

How can so much life exist where there is so little food or sunlight? Many creatures transform chemicals from the vents into food. This process is called chemosynthesis. Creatures that don't use chemosynthesis, such as crabs, eat the ones that do.

In the last few decades, scientists have discovered more than 1,500 ocean species! If sea exploration continues, then they will discover many more.

Mussels, worms, and crabs live near vents.

OAR/National Undersea Research Program (NURP)/Texas A&M Univ/NOAA

Make Connections

Talk about how sea creatures adapt to the deep ocean. **ESSENTIAL QUESTION**

Compare how sea creatures adapt with another animal that you know. **TEXT TO SELF**

Text Evidence

1 Specific Vocabulary Ⓐ Ⓒ Ⓣ

The word *teem* means "be full of." Underline context clues that tell about the meaning. How do you know the vents teem with life?

I know the vents teem with life

because _____

_____.

2 Sentence Structure Ⓐ Ⓒ Ⓣ

Reread the second sentence of the third paragraph. Circle what chemicals transform into. What is this called?

It is called _____

_____.

3 Comprehension
Cause and Effect

Reread the last sentence. Put a box around the effect of exploration. Write about it.

_____ will discover many

more _____.

Respond to the Text

Partner Discussion Work with a partner. Read the questions about "Mysterious Oceans." Show where you found text evidence. Write the page numbers. Then discuss what you learned.

How have creatures in the deep ocean adapted?

I read that the ocean floor is _____.

Deep sea starfish adapted by _____.

Anglerfish adapted by _____.

Text Evidence

Page(s): _____

Page(s): _____

Page(s): _____

What did scientists discover near the vents on the ocean floor?

I read that the bottom of the ocean is teeming with _____.

The creatures that live around the vents are _____

_____.

Sea creatures there transform chemicals into _____.

Text Evidence

Page(s): _____

Page(s): _____

Page(s): _____

Group Discussion Present your answers to the group. Cite text evidence for your ideas. Listen to and discuss the group's opinions.

Write Work with a partner. Look at your notes about "Mysterious Oceans." Write your answer to the Essential Question. Use text evidence to support your answer. Use vocabulary words in your writing.

How are sea creatures adapted in the deep ocean?

Deep sea starfish adapted by _____

_____.

Anglerfish adapted by _____

_____.

The creatures that live near the vents adapted by _____

_____.

Share Writing Present your writing to the class. Discuss their opinions. Talk about their ideas. You can say:

I agree with _____.

I do not agree because _____.

Write to Sources

Ana

Take Notes About the Text I took notes about the text on the idea web to answer the question: *Why do deep-sea animals have adaptations? Use text evidence.*

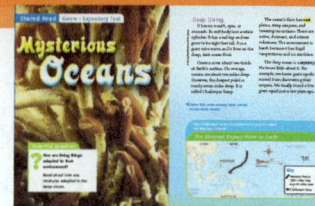

pages 32–35

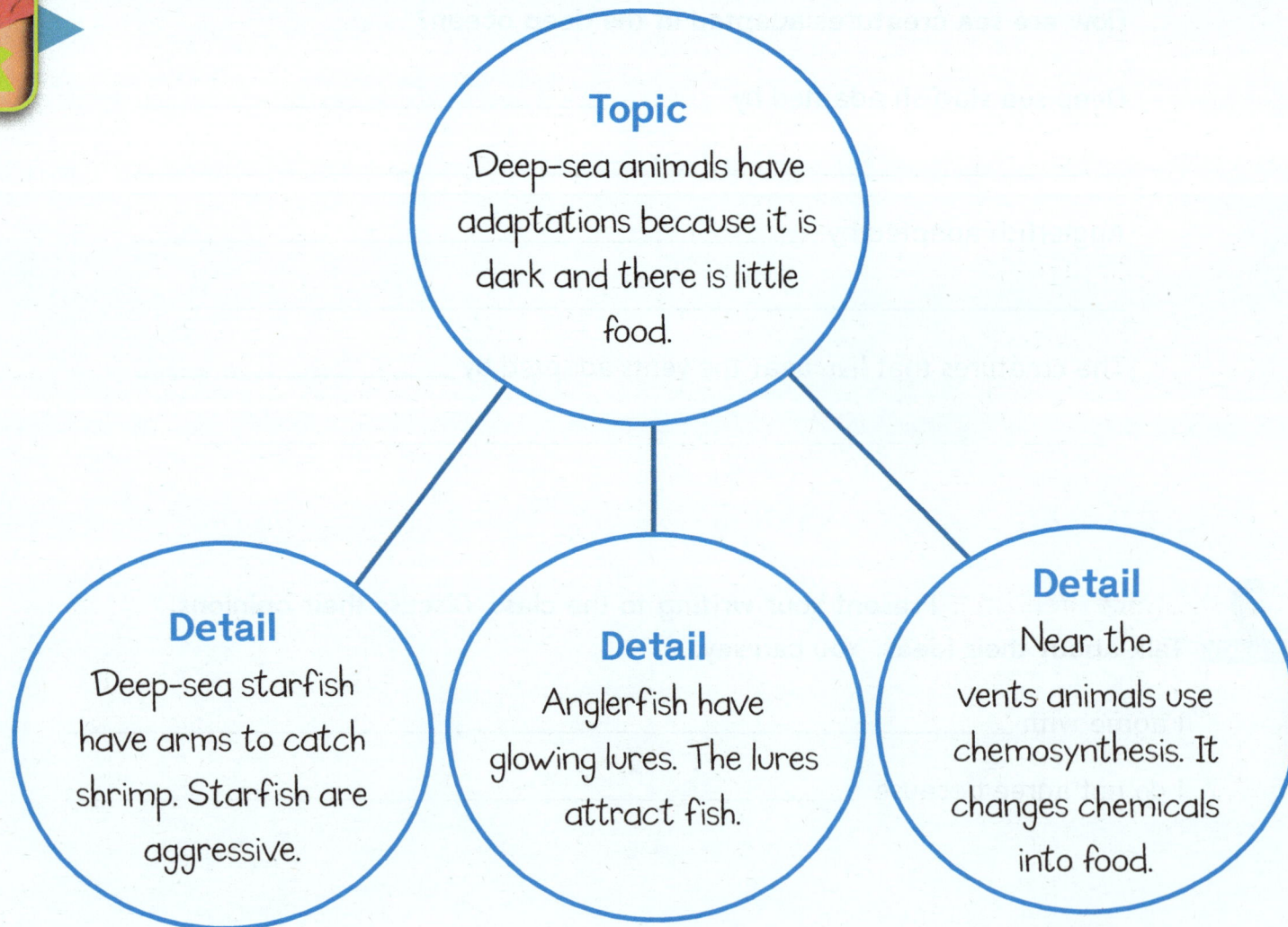

Topic
Deep-sea animals have adaptations because it is dark and there is little food.

Detail
Deep-sea starfish have arms to catch shrimp. Starfish are aggressive.

Detail
Anglerfish have glowing lures. The lures attract fish.

Detail
Near the vents animals use chemosynthesis. It changes chemicals into food.

Write About the Text I used notes from my idea web to write a paragraph about deep-sea animals.

Student Model: *Informative Text*

Deep-sea animals have adaptations because the bottom of the ocean is cold and has very little food. Deep-sea starfish are aggressive. They use their arms to catch shrimp. Anglerfish have glowing lures. They use their arms to attract and catch fish. Near the vents animals use chemosynthesis. It changes chemicals into food. These adaptations help the animals to live at the bottom of the deep ocean.

TALK ABOUT IT

Text Evidence
Draw a box around a sentence that comes from the notes. Did Ana use the information as a detail?

Grammar
Circle an irregular noun. How is an irregular noun different from a regular noun?

Connect Ideas
Underline the two sentences about deep-sea starfish. How can you combine the sentences and connect the ideas?

Your Turn
COLLABORATE

Explain the adaptations of the animals living around deep-sea vents.

>> Go Digital!
Write your response online. Use your editing checklist.

? **Essential Question**
What impact do our actions have on our world?

>> *Go Digital*

40

What is the man doing to take care of the chimpanzees? How does he make a difference? What do people do to make a difference? Write words in the chart.

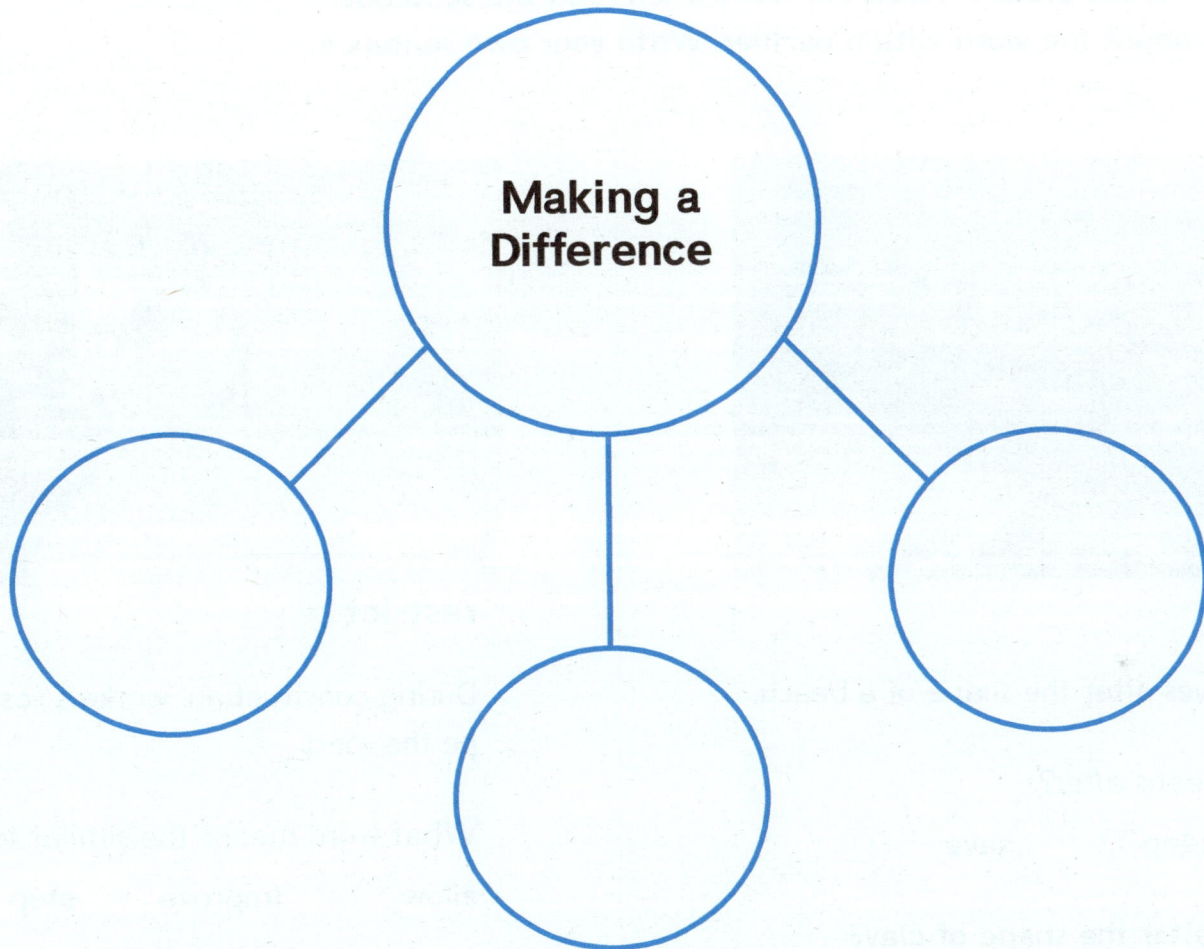

Making a Difference

Discuss what people do to make a difference. Use words from the chart. You can say:

The man is _____ to take care of the chimpanzees.

To make a difference, people _____.

More Vocabulary

COLLABORATE

Look at the picture. Read the word. Then read the sentence.
Talk about the word with a partner. Write your own sentence.

alter

Over time, waves **alter** the shape of a beach.

What word means *alter*?

change   **keep**   **save**

How can you alter the shape of clay?

I can alter the shape of clay by

_____.

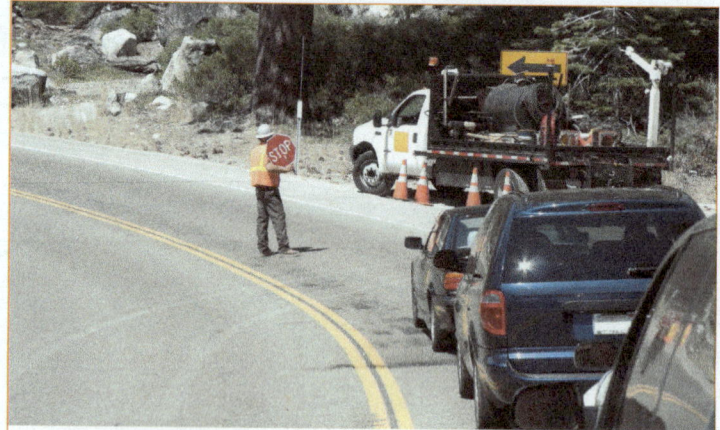

restrict

During construction, workers **restrict** driving on the road.

What word means the similar to *restrict*?

allow   **improve**   **stop**

How do traffic lights restrict people?

Traffic lights restrict people by

_____.

42

Words and Phrases: *throughout* and *while*

The word *throughout* means "from beginning to end."

How long did it rain?

It rained **throughout** the day.

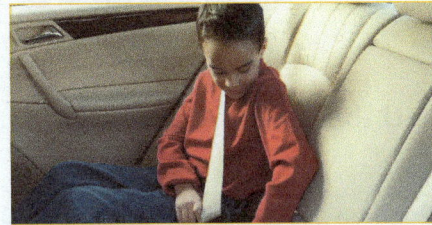

The word *while* means "during the time something happens."

When does Katrina wear a seatbelt?

Katrina wears a seatbelt **while** she is riding in a car.

COLLABORATE Look at the picture. Read the sentence. Talk with a partner. Write the phrase that completes each sentence.

Jeff and Lucy slept _____

the movie.

throughout while

Lizzie waits _____

her friends finish the video game.

throughout while

Sash Alexander Photography/Moment Open/Getty Images; Eclipse Studios/McGraw-Hill Education; Onoky Photography/SuperStock; DreamPictures/Photodisc/Getty Images

COLLABORATE

1 Talk About It

Look at the photograph. Read the title. Discuss what you see. Use these words.

save   world   observe   nature

Write about what you see.

The text is about _____

_____.

Who is the person in the photograph?

The person in the photograph is

_____

_____.

What information does the caption tell you about the photograph?

Rachel Carson liked to _____

_____.

Take notes as you read the text.

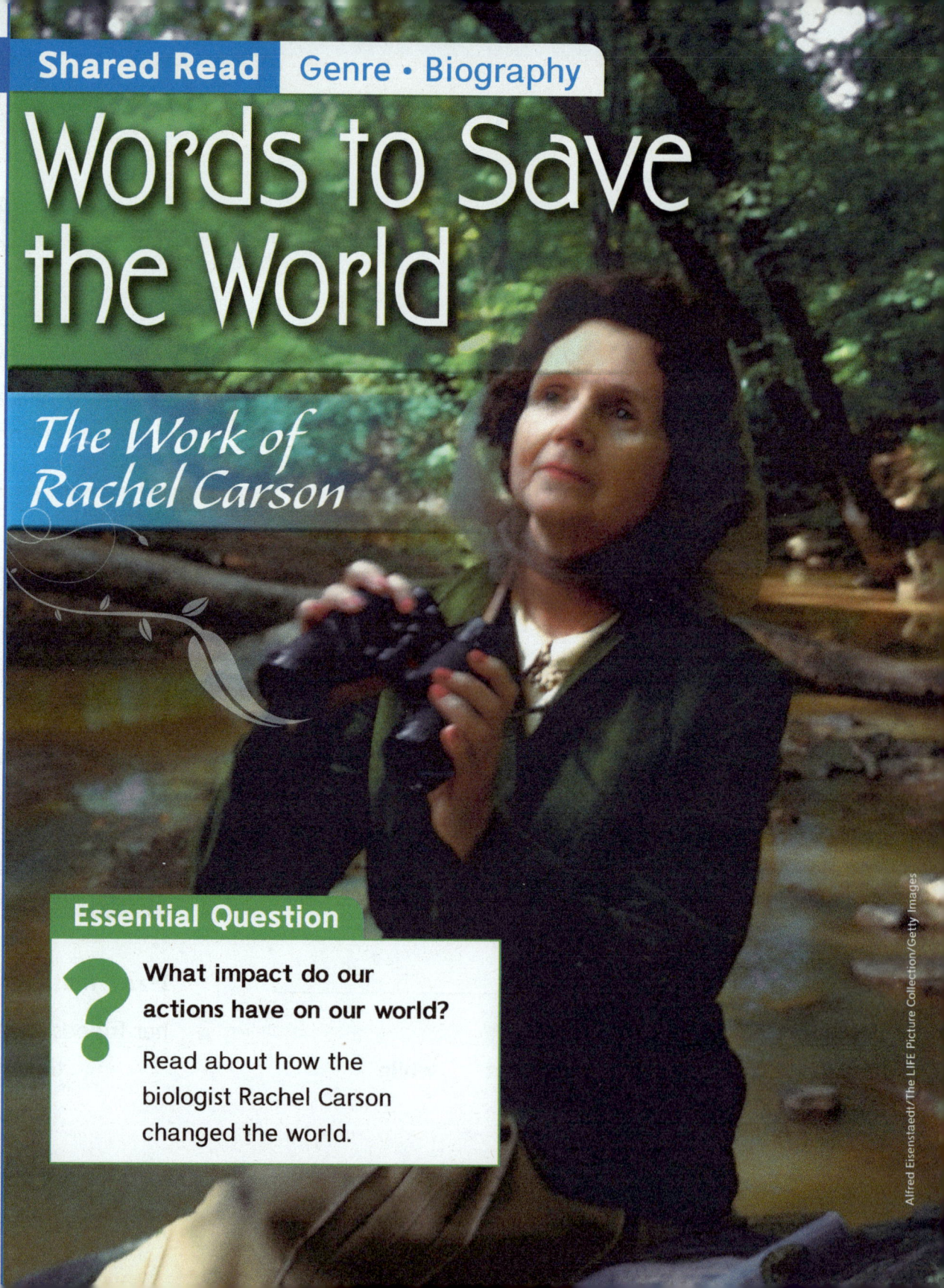

Words to Save the World

The Work of Rachel Carson

Essential Question

?

What impact do our actions have on our world?

Read about how the biologist Rachel Carson changed the world.

Alfred Eisenstaedt/The LIFE Picture Collection/Getty Images

Sometimes, the quietest voice can spark the most clamorous outrage. Rachel Carson was a soft-spoken writer who loved nature. Her work helped the U.S. government strengthen the rules and regulations on the use of pesticides. Many people consider Rachel's book *Silent Spring* the foundation of today's environmental movement.

Early Years

Rachel was born in Springdale, Pennsylvania, in 1907. Throughout her childhood, she explored the land around her family's farm and developed a love of nature. She studied biology in college. While studying at a marine laboratory, Rachel became fascinated by the sea.

◀ Rachel preferred to gather information alone.

From an early age, Rachel loved to write. She began her career by writing radio programs for the U.S. Bureau of Fisheries. Then she became an editor and librarian for the agency. She also submitted articles to newspapers and magazines. Rachel eventually published three books about the ocean. The trilogy included *Under the Sea-Wind, The Sea Around Us,* and *The Edge of the Sea.*

Rachel supported her ideas with facts.

Alfred Eisenstaedt/The LIFE Picture Collection/Getty Images

Text Evidence

1 Specific Vocabulary A C T

The word *spark* means "to cause something to happen." Circle the result that the quietest voice sparks. Rewrite the sentence using a different word for *spark*.

_____

_____

2 Comprehension

Reread the first paragraph. Underline the effects of Rachel Carson's work. Write about it.

Rachel Carson's work helped to

_____

_____.

3 Sentence Structure A C T

Reread the third sentence of the last paragraph. What does the agency refer to? Put a box around the text.

The agency is _____.

Text Evidence

1 Comprehension

Problem and Solution

Reread the first paragraph. Underline a solution to the problem of insects eating crops. What new problem did the solution cause?

The new problem was _____

_____.

2 Sentence Structure A C T

Reread first and second sentences of the last paragraph. Circle text in the first sentence that the second sentence tells about.

_____

_____

3 Talk About It

Reread the last paragraph. Discuss what Rachel probably said when she testified. Use text evidence to support your answer.

Rachel's research revealed that DDT damaged birds and their eggs.

A Call for Help

One day Rachel received a letter from friends, Olga and Stuart Huckins. They described the problems they had from spraying DDT on their wildlife sanctuary. Chemical companies had developed DDT as a solution to crop-eating insects. However, the DDT seemed to harm birds at the sanctuary.

In response, Rachel researched the Huckins's claim and published her findings. She hoped to warn about the dangers of DDT. She urged readers to imagine a world without songbirds. Her book, *Silent Spring*, describes the result of using many pesticides.

Silent Spring prompted readers to raise their voices in unison. People wanted the government to **restrict** the use of pesticides. Rachel testified before a Congressional committee and provided facts and information to influence their decisions.

Animals also feel the effects of pesticides.

(l) James P. Blair/National Geographic/Getty Images; (r) Alfred Eisenstaedt/Time & Life Pictures/Getty Images

Sample Food Chains

TROPHIC LEVEL	GRASSLAND BIOME	OCEAN BIOME
Primary Producer	grass	phytoplankton
Primary Consumer	grasshopper	zooplankton
Secondary Consumer	rat	fish
Tertiary Consumer	snake	seal

A Strong Reaction

Meanwhile, the chemical companies struggled to argue against Rachel. They tried to label her ideas as irrational. They mocked her writing style and made fun of her ideas. Their TV advertisements claimed the safety of their products. These ads did not change public opinion, however.

Rachel worried that there would be no solution when pesticides poisoned an area. She thought it might be impossible to restore the environment to its original state. She said that people "have now acquired a fateful power to **alter** and destroy nature." Her testimony led the U.S. government to restrict some pesticides in this country.

Rachel Carson died shortly after *Silent Spring* was published, but her voice survives within her books. Her love of nature endures, along with her quiet desire to preserve and protect the natural world.

Carson understood the power her words had on children.

Alfred Eisenstaedt/The LIFE Picture Collection/Getty Images

Make Connections

? What impact did Rachel's book *Silent Spring* have on the makers of pesticides?
ESSENTIAL QUESTION

Think about a time when you spoke out about something. What impact did your words have?
TEXT TO SELF

Text Evidence

1 Comprehension
Problem and Solution

Reread the first paragraph. Did the chemical companies find a solution to their problem? Underline the text that tells you. Write about it.

The chemical companies _____

_____.

2 Specific Vocabulary A C T

The word *survives* means "to continue to live." Circle another word that has a similar meaning in the second sentence.

COLLABORATE

3 Talk About It

Reread the last paragraph. Discuss the meaning of the phrase *her voice survives within her books*. Then write about it.

Her voice survives by _____

_____.

Respond to the Text

Partner Discussion Work with a partner. Read the questions about "Words to Save the World." Show where you found text evidence. Write the page numbers. Then discuss what you learned.

What effects did pesticides have on the environment?

Text Evidence 🔍

Chemical companies developed pesticides to_____.

Page(s): _____

Pesticides solved the problem by _____.

Page(s): _____

Pesticides also harmed _____.

Page(s): _____

What did Rachel Carson do about the use of pesticides?

Text Evidence 🔍

Rachel Carson wrote a book to_____.

Page(s): _____

She also testified to _____.

Page(s): _____

As a result, the government _____

Page(s): _____

_____.

Group Discussion Present your answers to the group. Cite text evidence for your ideas. Listen to and discuss the group's opinions.

Write Work with a partner. Look at your notes about "Words to Save the World." Write your answer to the Essential Question. Use text evidence to support your answer. Use vocabulary words in your writing.

What effects did Rachel Carson's actions have on the environment?

Rachel Carson's work inspired people to _____

_____.

As a result, the government restricted _____

_____

_____.

Rachel's actions helped to _____

_____.

Share Writing Present your writing to the class. Discuss their opinions. Talk about their ideas. You can say:

I agree with _____.

I do not agree because _____.

Write to Sources

Yasmine

Take Notes About the Text I took notes about the text on the chart to answer the question: *In your opinion, is the author against pesticides? Use text evidence.*

pages 44–47

Details	Point of View
Author tells that Rachel did research for information. Author tells that Rachel wrote about her discoveries. Author tells good and bad things about pesticides. Author tells the government investigated pesticides. The government restricted some pesticides.	The author is not against pesticides. The author describes why the government restricted some pesticides.

Write About the Text I used notes from my chart to write an opinion.

Student Model: *Opinion*

The author is not against pesticides. The author tells about Rachel Carson. She researched about pesticides. She wrote about her discoveries. The author tells good things about pesticides. The author tells bad things about pesticides. Then, the author describes how the government investigated pesticides. As a result, the government restricted some pesticides. The text tells what happened to pesticides. It does not tell that the author is against pesticides.

TALK ABOUT IT

COLLABORATE

Text Evidence
Draw a box around a sentence that comes from the notes. Does Yasmine use the information as a supporting detail?

Grammar
Circle the pronoun in the last sentence. What does this pronoun refer to?

Condense Ideas
Underline the sentences that tell about what the author wrote about pesticides. How can you use *and* to condense the sentences into one sentence?

Your Turn

COLLABORATE

In your opinion, should the governments in all countries ban DDT? Use text evidence in your writing.

≫ *Go Digital!*
Write your response online. Use your editing checklist.

TALK ABOUT IT

Weekly Concept Out in the World

 **Essential Question**

What can our connections to the world teach us?

>> *Go Digital*

52

What is the boy doing? What does the boy do to stay connected to his family, friends, and the world? How do people stay connected to the world? Write words in the chart.

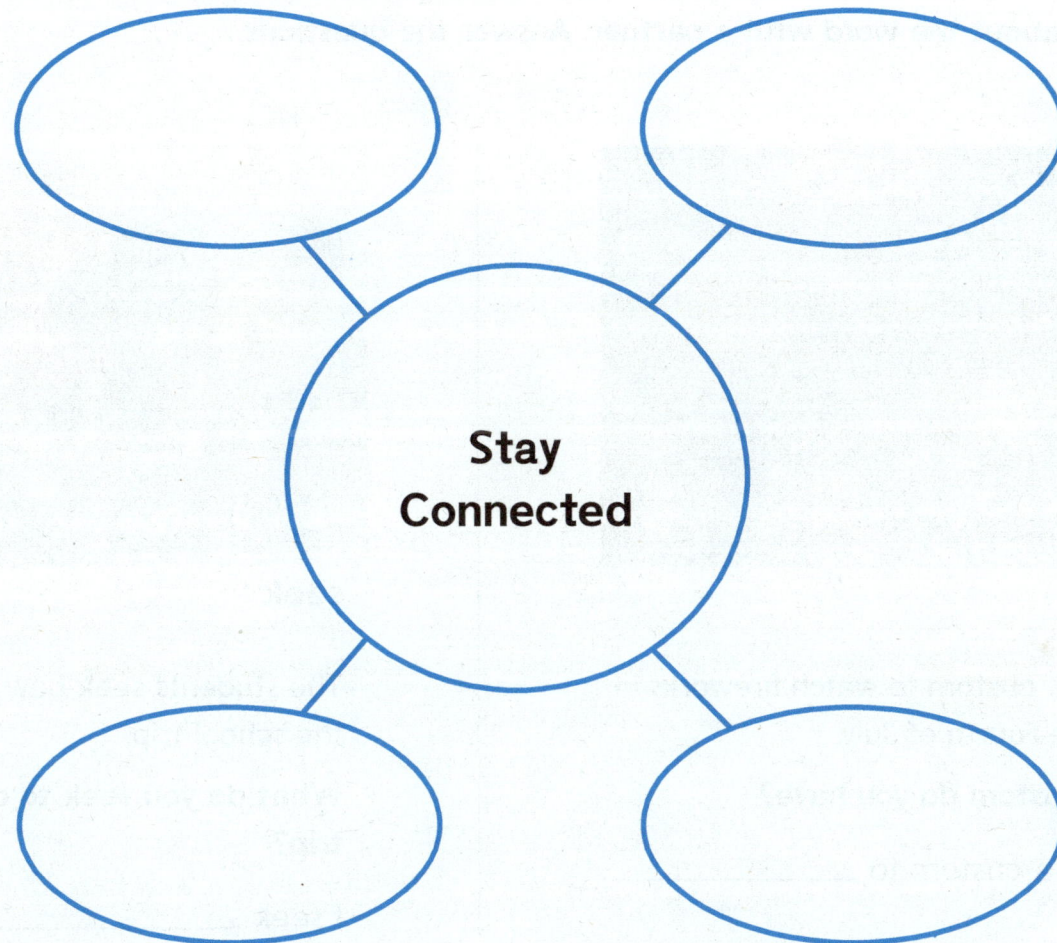

Stay Connected

Discuss how people stay connected to the world. Use words from the chart. Complete the sentences.

The boy is _____ to stay connected.

People stay connected by _____.

More Vocabulary

Look at the picture. Read the word. Then read the sentence.
Talk about the word with a partner. Answer the questions.

customs

My family has a **custom** to watch fireworks in the park on the Fourth of July.

What family custom do you have?

My family has a custom to _____

_____.

seek

The students **seek** new experiences during the school trip.

What do you seek to do during a family trip?

I seek _____

during a family trip.

Poetry Terms

imagery

Imagery creates pictures in a reader's mind.

The trees wave as I race by.

---

personification

Personification describes objects, animals, or ideas as people.

The thunder clapped through the night.

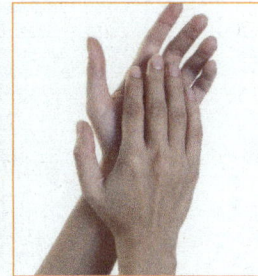

COLLABORATE

Work with a partner. Choose the best word that shows personification. Use the words below. Say them together.

calling   **crawl**

wink   **yells**

My alarm clock

_____ at me.

The slow cars

_____ along.

The stars _____ at me.

That juicy plum is

_____ my name.

COLLABORATE

① Talk About It

Look at the photograph. Discuss what you see. Then write about it. Use these words.

house   hills   trees   country

I see _____.

It is in the _____

_____.

② Literary Element
Personification

Reread lines 5–6 of the second stanza. Circle an example of personification.

③ Specific Vocabulary Ⓐ Ⓒ Ⓣ

The word *scenes* means "views or pictures." Underline the text that tells who is speaking. Why did the speaker say this?

To Travel!

To travel! To travel!
To visit distant places;
To leave my corner of the world
To **seek** new names and faces.
Adventure! Adventure!
Exploring foreign lands;
If I can leap across the globe,
My universe expands!

A novel waves her arms to me,
"Come read! Come read!" she cries.
Her pages dance with ancient tales,
A feast for hungry eyes!
The paintings on museum walls
Are begging me to tour:
"Leave your home and live our **scenes**,
A grand exchange for sure!"

Essential Question

? **What can our connections to the world teach us?**

Read a poem about connecting with other cultures.

To travel! To travel!
Through timeless books and art,
I enter and experience
A life so far apart.

I sail across the seven seas,
My heart soars like a bird.
And soon I'm hearing languages
I've never, ever heard.

Far across the seven seas,
Aromas fill the air.
Foods I've never, ever tried
Are eaten everywhere!
Music blares a different tune,
And strange, new clothes are worn.
Parents pass on customs
To the young ones who are born.

I've traveled! I've traveled!
It's left me more aware;
A valuable connection
To the universe we share.
By reading books and viewing art,
I've learned a thing or two:
The world was made not just for me,
But made for me and you!

— Jad Abbas

Make Connections

? Talk about how the speaker connects to the world through books and art. **ESSENTIAL QUESTION**

What do you do to feel connected to the world? **TEXT TO SELF**

Text Evidence

1 Comprehension
Point of View

Reread the first stanza. How does the speaker travel? Circle the text that tells you.

The speaker travels by _____

_____.

2 Specific Vocabulary ACT

Aromas are smells. What aromas fill the air? Circle the text that tells you.

Aromas are from _____

COLLABORATE

3 Talk About It

Explain how reading is like traveling. Put a box around the text that tells you. Write about it.

Through books and art, the speaker

learns about _____

_____.

Respond to the Text

Partner Discussion Work with a partner. Read the questions about "To Travel!" Show where you found text evidence. Write the page numbers. Then discuss what you read.

COLLABORATE

How does the speaker connect to the world?

I read that the speaker visits _____.

He travels through _____.

He makes a connection to the _____.

Text Evidence

Page(s): _____

Page(s): _____

Page(s): _____

What does the speaker learn?

The speaker hears _____.

He is introduced to new _____.

The speaker learns to connect with _____.

Text Evidence

Page(s): _____

Page(s): _____

Page(s): _____

Group Discussion Present your answers to the group. Cite text evidence for your ideas. Listen to and discuss the group's opinions.

COLLABORATE

Write Work with a partner. Look at your notes about "To Travel!" Write your answer to the Essential Question. Use text evidence to support your answer. Use vocabulary words in your writing.

What do the speaker's connections to the world teach him?

The speaker connects to the world by _____.

_____

_____.

The speaker learns that _____

_____.

Share Writing Present your writing to the class. Discuss their opinions. Talk about their ideas. You can say:

I agree with _____.

I do not agree because _____.

Write to Sources

Frank

Take Notes About the Text I took notes about the text on the chart to answer the prompt: *Write about how the poet uses personification in the poem.*

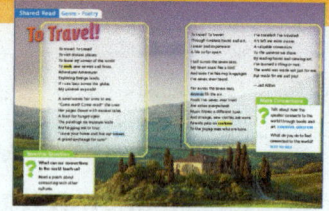

pages 56–57

Text Clues

A novel waves her arms to me,

"Come read! Come read!" she cries.

Her pages dance with ancient tales,"

What You Know

A novel can't wave arms. People wave arms.

A novel can't talk. People can talk.

"Her pages" refers to the pages in the novel.

Pages can't dance. People dance. When people dance, they are full of life.

Inferences

The poet uses personification to tell about a book. The poet tells that the pages of a novel are full of life.

Write About the Text I used notes from my chart to write an informative paragraph.

Student Model: *Informative Text*

In the poem "To Travel!", the poet uses personification to describe a novel. The poet wrote, "A novel waves her arms to me, 'Come read! Come read!' she cries. Her pages dance with ancient tales." The poet tells about the novel as a person. The novel waves its arms. The novel talks. The pages dance. When people dance, they're full of life. The poet is saying the stories in novels are full of life.

TALK ABOUT IT

Text Evidence

Draw a box around a sentence that comes from the notes. Does Frank use the information as a supporting detail?

Grammar

Circle the text that comes from the poem. Why is the text surrounded by quotation marks?

Condense Ideas

Underline the two sentences that tell what the novel does like a person. How can you use *and* to condense the sentences into one sentence?

Your Turn

Explain another example of personification in the poem. Use text evidence in your writing.

>> *Go Digital!*
Write your response online. Use your editing checklist.